LOVE

Is a Four-Legged Word

Wit and Wisdom for Pet Lovers

Steve Burt

LOVE

Is a Four-Legged Word

Wit and Wisdom for Pet Lovers

Steve Burt

ISBN 978-0-9856188-9-6
Burt Creations imprint
Cover: SelfPubBookCovers.com/Viergacht
www.SteveBurtBooks.com

For information:
Steve Burt
17101 SE 94th Berrien Court
The Villages, FL 32162

ALL YOU NEED IS LOVE...
AND A CAT!

In this house, cat hair is a fashion accessory and a condiment.

A HOUSE IS NOT A HOME
WITHOUT A CAT

And God Created Cat

On the first day of Creation God created the cat.

On the second day God created the human to serve the cat.

On the third day God created tuna, mice, and all the animals of the earth to serve as potential food for the cat.

Wit and Wisdom for Pet Lovers

On the fourth day God created honest toil so that the human could labor for the good of the cat.

On the fifth day God created the ball of yarn, the feather thingie on a string, and the catnip mouse so that the cat might or might not be amused.

On the sixth day God created veterinary science to keep the cat healthy and the human broke.

On the seventh day God tried to rest, but the cat woke God up at 5 a.m.

Never leave home without a kiss and a hug, and an 'I love you.' Then remove the dog hair from your mouth as you walk to the car.

LOVE MY FUR BABY.

"My fashion philosophy is, if you're not covered in dog hair, your life is empty."
– Elayne Boosler

Home is where the dogs are.

You, me, and the dog.
Stay pawsitive.

Dog mother, wine lover.

Never underestimate the
therapeutic power of talking to
your dog every day while having
a glass of wine.

*Is it normal to like dogs more
than people? Asking for a friend.*

Accidentally used the dog's shampoo today and I'm feeling like such a good girl.

Dog hair, don't care

"Anybody who doesn't know what soap tastes like never washed a dog."
–Franklin P. Jones

All guests must be approved by the dog!

Rescued is my favorite breed.

IF OUR DOG DOESN'T LIKE YOU
– WE PROBABLY WON'T EITHER

Dogs – because people suck.

"Money can buy you a fine dog, but only love can make him wag his tail."
– Kinky Friedman

I prefer dogs over people.

Adopt, don't shop.

**Pets welcome,
people tolerated.**

"SCRATCH A DOG AND YOU'LL
FIND A PERMANENT JOB."
– FRANKLIN P. JONES

Cat mom

Always room for one more cat

Cats are not our whole life, but they make our life whole.

"The greatness of a nation and its moral progress can be judged by the way its animals are treated."
-Mahatma Gandhi

I want all the dogs.

Be the person
your dog thinks you are.

A house is not a home
without paw prints.

"When the dog looks at you, the dog is not thinking what kind of a person you are. The dog is not judging you." – Eckhart Tolle

Nothing better than naps with the dog.

A wagging tail and a friendly woof bring joy to all beneath this roof.

"Such short little lives our pets have to spend with us, and they spend most of it waiting for us to come home each day."
–John Grogan

Happiness is being owned by a cat.

I WORK SO MY CAT CAN HAVE A BETTER LIFE.

The cat rules this house.

You lost me at "I don't like cats."

"You cannot look at a sleeping cat and feel tense."
-Jane Pauley

Wit and Wisdom for Pet Lovers

No outfit is complete
without cat hair.

Wet kisses, cold noses, wagging
tails. You had us at woof and meow.

"Pets reflect you like mirrors.
When you are happy, you can see
your dog smiling and when you
are sad, your cat cries."
Munia Khan, Bangladeshi Poet

If my dogs make you uncomfortable, I'm happy to lock you in another room.

Beware of the dog, don't trust the cat either.

Home is wherever my dog is.

"If there are no dogs in Heaven, then when I die I want to go where they went." –Will Rogers

Live like someone left the gate open.

The road to my heart is paved with paw prints.

**"If I have any beliefs about immortality, it is that certain dogs I have known will go to heaven, and very, very few persons."
—James Thurber**

Wit and Wisdom for Pet Lovers

No soliciting – ask dog for details.

My dog is my doorbell

Love is a four-legged word.

You can't buy love, but you can rescue it.

"The average dog is a nicer person than the average person."
–Andy Rooney

"The more people I meet the more I like my dog."

Home is where the cat hair sticks to everything but the cat.

Time spent with cats is never wasted.

Some angels have wings, mine have tails.

"I don't understand people who don't touch their pets. Their cat or dog is called a pet for a reason."
–Jarod Kintz

A spoiled cat lives here.

**Dogs have owners,
cats have staff.**

One cat leads to another.

"Indeed, there is nothing on this
earth more peaceful than a
sleeping, purring cat."
-Jonathon Scott Payne

**"Sometimes, your pet picks
you."
-Julie Wenzel**

Love is wet noses, slobbery kisses, and a wagging tail.

Wag more, bark less.

"Recruit your pet as a study partner. Cats are usually more than happy to do this—in fact, you may have trouble keeping them off keyboards and books—and dogs will often serve as well. Few things are more relaxing than having a warm, furry creature next to you as you study."
-Stefanie Weisman

It's impossible to keep a straight face in the presence of one or more puppies.

"If it wasn't for puppies, some people would never go for a walk."

"Happiness is a warm puppy."
–Charles Shultz

"Every puppy should have a boy."
–Erma Bombeck

"Pets bring vital energy to our homes and lives. Pets communicate many messages about love and connection. Care tenderly for all pets throughout their precious lives."

"The best way to get a puppy is to beg for a baby brother– and they'll settle for a puppy every time."
–Winston Pendleton

"No one appreciates the very special genius of your conversation as the dog does."
–Christopher Morley

Dog is God spelled backward.

"A dog is the only thing on earth that loves you more than you love yourself."

–Josh Billings

I WOULD RATHER BE CALLED THE CAT LADY THAN A PEOPLE PERSON.

Best friends are ones with paws.

Cats leave paw prints in your heart, forever and always.

"Cats have it all – admiration, an endless sleep, and company only when they want it."
-Rod McKuen

"I just want to be in my sweats, walk my dog, watch TV and eat pizza."
–America Ferrera

"When the Man waked up, he said, 'What is Wild Dog doing here?' And the Woman said, 'His name is not Wild Dog anymore but the First Friend, because he will be our friend for always and always and always.'"
-Rudyard Kipling

"Everything I know,
I learned from dogs."
–Nora Roberts

Wit and Wisdom for Pet Lovers

And so the snuggles and treats
begin.

WHAT GREATER GIFT THAN THE LOVE OF A CAT?

**"Time spent with cats is
never wasted."
-Sigmund Freud**

**"Cats are connoisseurs of comfort."
-James Herriot**

Wit and Wisdom for Pet Lovers

"The dog is the god of frolic."
–Henry Ward Beecher

"The most affectionate creature in
the world is a wet dog."
-Charles Dickens

"What do dogs do on their
day off? Can't lie around –
that's their job."
–George Carlin

Life is too short to just have one dog.

"MY LITTLE DOG –
A HEARTBEAT AT MY FEET."
–EDITH WHARTON

"Outside of a dog, a book is a man's best friend. Inside of a dog it's too dark to read."
–Groucho Marx

"Dogs laugh, but they laugh with their tails."
-Max Eastman

"When you adopt a dog, you have a lot of very good days and one very bad day."
–W. Bruce Cameron

"If you have a dog, you will most likely outlive it; to get a dog is to open yourself to profound joy and, prospectively, to equally profound sadness."
–Marjorie Garber

Home is where the dog runs to greet you.

"There is no psychiatrist in the world like a puppy licking your face."
-Ben Williams, Jazz Musician

"Dogs and angels are not very far apart."
-Charles Bukowski

Wit and Wisdom for Pet Lovers

"There's a saying. If you want someone to love you forever, buy a dog, feed it and keep it around."
–Dick Dale

"You want a friend in Washington? Get a dog."
–Harry S Truman

"It's tough to stay married. My wife kisses the dogs on the lips, yet she won't drink from my glass."
-Rodney Dangerfield

When the cat you love becomes a memory, the memory becomes a treasure.

"Pets are humanizing. They remind us we have an obligation and responsibility to preserve and nurture and care for all life."
-James Cromwell, actor

"I had been told that the training procedure with cats was difficult. It's not. Mine had me trained in two days."
-Bill Dana, comedian

Whoever said that diamonds are a girl's best friend never owned a dog.

"My idea of absolute happiness is to be in bed on a rainy day with my blankie, my cat, and my dog."
-Anne Lamott, writer

"No matter how little money and how few possessions you own, having a dog makes you feel rich."
Louis Sabin, author

My sunshine doesn't come from the sky. It comes from the love in my dog's eyes.

"You do not own a dog. You have a dog. And the dog has you."
-Chelsea Handler

"Dogs are the leaders of the planet. If you see two life forms, one of them's making a poop, the other one's carrying it for him, who would you assume is in charge?"
-Jerry Seinfeld

Every cat is my best friend.

"It is impossible for a lover of cats to banish these alert, gentle, and discriminating friends, who give us just enough of their regard and complaisance to make us hunger for more."
-Agnes Repplier

"My cats inspire me daily. They inspire me to get a dog!"
-Greg Curtis

"No matter how much cats fight, there always seem to be plenty of kittens."
-Abraham Lincoln

"The truth is that it's just really hard for me to get to sleep without a dog in my bedroom."
-Jimmy Stewart

**"A boy can learn a lot from a dog: obedience, loyalty, and the importance of turning around three times before lying down."
-Robert Benchley**

"Don't accept your dog's admiration as conclusive evidence that you are wonderful."

-Ann Landers

"Histories are more full of examples of the fidelity of dogs than of friends."
-Alexander Pope

"Until one has loved an animal, a part
of one's soul remains unawakened."
-Anatole France

"YOU KNOW, A DOG CAN SNAP
YOU OUT OF ANY KIND OF BAD
MOOD THAT YOU'RE IN FASTER
THAN YOU CAN THINK OF."
-JILL ABRAMSON, EDITOR

"Petting, scratching, and
cuddling a dog could be as
soothing to the mind and heart
as deep meditation and almost
as good for the soul as prayer."
-Dean Koontz

"I am fond of pigs. Dogs look up to us. Cats look down on us. Pigs treat us as equals."
-Winston Churchill

"Way down deep, we're all motivated by the same urges. Cats have the courage to live by them."
- Jim Davis

"I have felt cats rubbing their faces against mine and touching my cheek with claws carefully sheathed. These things, to me, are expressions of love."
-James Herriot

My dog thinks I'm a catch.

"If I could be half the person my dog is, I'd be twice the human I am."
-Charles Yu, author

"When a man's best friend is his dog, that dog has a problem."
–Edward Abbey

"Just watching my cats can make me happy."
-Paula Cole

"It's difficult to understand why people don't realize that pets are gifts to humankind."
-Linda Blair

"You think dogs will not be in heaven? I tell you, they will be there long before any of us."
–Robert Louis Stevenson

Wit and Wisdom for Pet Lovers

"Whoever said you can't buy
happiness forgot little puppies."
-Gene Hill

"It seems to me that the good Lord
in his infinite wisdom gave us three
things to make life bearable—
hope, jokes, and dogs. But the
greatest of these was dogs."
-Robyn Davidson

**"Some of our greatest historical
and artistic treasures we place
with curators in museums;
others we take for walks."
-Roger Caras**

Thousands of years ago, cats were worshiped as gods. Cats have never forgotten this.

"Cats are smarter than dogs. You can't get eight cats to pull a sled through snow."
–Jeff Valdez

"Cats are intended to teach us that not everything in nature has a purpose."
-Garrison Keillor

Best part of the day is coming home to a wagging tail.

"When you feel lousy, puppy therapy is indicated."
-Sarah Paretsky, mystery writer

"Thorns may hurt you, men desert you, sunlight turn to fog; but you're never friendless ever if you have a dog."
-Douglas Malloch

Who loves me will love my dog also.

"Old age means realizing you will never own all the dogs you wanted to."
-Joe Gores

"People have been asking me if I was going to have kids, and I had puppies instead."
-Kate Jackson

"A LOT OF SHELTER DOGS ARE MUTTS LIKE ME."
-BARACK OBAMA

Keep calm and pet a dog.

"FOLKS WILL KNOW HOW
LARGE YOUR SOUL IS BY THE
WAY YOU TREAT A DOG!"
-CHARLES F. DORAN

"A well-trained dog will make no
attempt to share your lunch. He
will just make you feel guilty so
that you cannot enjoy it."
-Helen Thomson

**"Life is a series of dogs."
-George Carlin**

Everyone thinks they have the best dog, and none of them are wrong.

"Ever consider what our dogs must think of us? I mean, here we come back from the grocery store with the most amazing haul— chicken, pork, half a cow. They must think we're the greatest hunters on earth!"
-Anne Tyler

"THE PHRASE 'DOMESTIC CAT'
IS AN OXYMORON."
-GEORGE WILL

"Owners of dogs will have noticed that, if you provide them with food and water and shelter and affection, they will think you are God. Whereas owners of cats are compelled to realize that, if you provide them with food and water and affection, they draw the conclusion that they are God."
-Christopher Hitchens

There are no bad days when you come home to a dog's love.

It's impossible to keep a straight face in the presence of one or more puppies.

"Dogs feel very strongly that they should always go with you in the car, in case the need should arise for them to bark violently at nothing, right in your ear."
-Dave Barry, humorist

"Cat's motto:
No matter what you've done wrong, always try to make it look like the dog did it."

The road to my heart is paved with paw prints.

All you need is love and a cat.

To err is human—to forgive, canine.

If you're lucky, a dog or cat will come into your life, steal your heart, and change everything.

"The more boys I meet,
the more I love my dog."
-Carrie Underwood

"In times of joy, all of us wished we
possessed a tail we could wag."
-W.H. Auden

The kindness one does for one
animal may not change the world
but it will change the world of that
one animal.

If you enjoyed *Love Is a Four-Legged Word*, try Steve Burt's *Dumb Jokes for Kids* series.

His teen detectives trilogy—*FreeK Camp, FreeK Show, FreeK Week*—won the Florida Book Festival Grand Prize and 4 Mom's Choice golds. His adult/teen novel, *The Bookseller's Daughter*, won N.Y. Book Festival Grand Prize.

A weird tales collection—*New England Seaside, Roadside, Graveside, Darkside*—won Best Young Adult at the Hollywood and New England Book Festivals.

His inspirational collection, *New England Christmas Sampler*, was named Best Spiritual at the New England Book Festival.

www.SteveBurtBooks.com

About the Author

Steve Burt's is a multi-genre writer whose many books include young adult/teen mysteries, adult thrillers, numerous ghost and weird tales collections, several inspirational collections, joke books, a collection of quotes for pet lovers, church leadership books, meditation collections, a canoeing guidebook, and more.

Dr. Burt's shorter writings have appeared in hundreds of venues like the ***Chicken Soup for the Soul*** books, ***Reader's Digest, Family Circle***, ***Down East, Yankee***, and ***Mature Living***.

The retired pastor/professor and his editor/wife Jolyn split their year between Wells, Maine and The Villages, Florida.

Made in the USA
Middletown, DE
29 May 2022